Poems from the Secret Place

☙❦❧

Christine A. O'Riley

*Selections to Honor the Wonder
of Life's Times and Seasons*

Copyright 2024 by Christine A. O'Riley

All rights reserved. No part of this publication may be reproduced, distributed, or transmitted in any form or by any means, including photocopying, recording, or other electronic or mechanical methods, without the prior written permission of the publisher, except in the case of brief quotations embodied in critical reviews and certain other noncommercial uses permitted by copyright law. For permission requests, write to the publisher, addressed "Attention: Permissions Coordinator," at the address below.

Celtic Cottage Press
162 Burben Way
Rochester, NY 14624

celticcottagepress24@gmail.com

Cover art by Christine M. McMullen, pen & ink with watercolor
"Birth-Flowers" by Designwork in Illustrations
Photo by Abigail Lynn Photography
Logo Design: Andrew Hakes
Library of Congress Number: 2024912380
Poems from the Secret Place / Christine A. O'Riley – First Edition
ISBN hardcover 978-1-7357980-3-5 | softcover 978-1-7357980-4-2 | eBook 978-1-7357980-5-9

Printed in the United States of America.

To Dick, my husband and the love
of my life through the times and seasons

Contents

Connected i
Greeting iii
Poems v

I. Springtimes 1
    The Secret Place 2
    Spring Equinox Song for the Geese 3
    COVID Daffodils 4
    Flowering Begins 5
    Cate 6
    Little Bird 7
    May 8
    Every May I Remember 9
    Flutter-Buzzing 10
    A Season in My Care 11
    Irene Tree 12
    I Am Privileged to Live in the Midst of a Bird Aviary 14
    Spring Cottage 16
    Evening Gratitude 17

II. Summering Seasons 19
    Good Night 20
    Hello Dear Summer 21
    And Summer 22

Summer Moment 23
Entry Point 24
Adirondack Woods 25
My Firefly Friend 26
Encounter at Montario Point 27
Loons 28
For Danny, Summer 1978 29
July Musings 30
Eyes of Earth 31
Lake Storm 32
Myriads of Meteorites 33
Grass Point Portrait 34
Firefly Sanctuary 35
Front Porch at Half-Moon 36
The Beckoning 37
August 38
Full-Term 39

III. Times of Autumn 41
September Woods 42
Raining Leaves 44
October Night Song 45
Somehow, I Have Always Known You 46
His Face 47
Autumnal Procession 48
Little Patrick 49
Wonder 50

Alex, Come and Rest a While 51
Solitary Star 52
He Rides on the Night..53
Majesty..54
For Kevin 55
The Piano 56
Into Their Times..58

IV. Winterings 59
Christmas Lights...60
Tale of Timothy 61
Adirondacks in Winter 62
Without a Sound..63
Jack the Cat..64
Into the Winter Woods 65
Hope Lay Just Below 66
Winter Sketch 67
Beneath January's Moon...68
Grandchildren Haiku 69
Musings at Midnight...70

About the Author 73
Acknowledgments 75

Connected

by Dick O'Riley

Dedicated to my wife
(A poem for the poet)

Unique, chosen, selected from above
A heart filled with wonder; a life kept by love
A mystery given favor to share with all her strength
Of heaven's golden goodness in measure without length.

The dawn will rise to kiss her lips, in search of her awake.
Soft winds go forth to share her words a promise will not break.
Clouds nor storms can keep her breath from halting hope's desire
Her passion thrust upon all doubt, consumed with holy fire.

I watch and wait and see her life unfold throughout the years
In love I gaze and now amazed my eyes do fill with tears
Considering I'm joined with her, her husband in this life
Connected to eternity with my woman, my love, my wife.

Greeting

Welcome, dear reader.

Throughout my life journey over the years, poems and reflections have found their way out of my heart and onto paper. In this my first volume of verse, I have collected bouquets of my writings that speak of times and seasons in the natural-spirit cycle of life. Woven together here are selections about nature and family with glimpses into my inner life.

Even the seemingly common and everyday can be honored and transformed into precious remembrances when looked upon from the secret place of the heart. It is a wonder how much can be contained within the smallest moments.

May you find in these pages a restful space to pause, reflect, and be refreshed. May you be inspired to linger in and pay attention to the moments in your life that call out to you. May you too find treasures of wonder there, as you look upon them from your own secret place.

Thank you for reading and lingering,

Chris

Poems

Poems are funny things.
They lie sleeping inside
hidden in the mystery
until a spirit breath
awakens them with a kiss,
and they flow out
all on their own
in such delight
to be born.

I. Springtimes

The Secret Place

It is where life's secrets are gently whispered. There, the genesis of being known by the Bright and Shining One comes alive to my childlike soul.

The wellspring of wonder is drawn up into my roots, opening these clay eyes to see intimate treasures in the everyday, springtime's flowers of remembrance along life's way . . .

It is where sacred imagination recreates with living words. In my lingering and noticing, dailiness is transformed into limitless vistas seen anew, from a hidden space of quietude and confidence.

There, destiny gestates. I know and am known. Dreams are released to breathe and take form as the timeless expression begins . . .
there, in the secret place.

Spring Equinox Song for the Geese

A bright welcoming sound
in sky's distance I hear,
the approach of the
harbinger's announcement here.

They bear in their bodies
a message so true,
departing in fall,
now, returning anew.

To proclaim to my heart
spring is near, hope is real!
The brightness of light
celebrates what I feel.

So my spirit leaps, sings, twirls;
my soul joins in too
as we dance and we dream
in what spring now makes new.

A calling V-presence above
me I now see,
sentinels of the equinox
bid me join them, flying free.

COVID Daffodils

The daffodils in radiance stand
Encircling yon apple tree, adorning the land.
With upturned faces they announce and decree
That all is well and love will be.
Amidst the tempest of the time,
They whisper now, "Spring is still mine."
When sad, I look to them and see
Bright reassurance promised me.
So, thank you God for daffodils true
That bloom for me
and make all things
new.

Flowering Begins

April evening
  and the breeze
    caresses my face
      with the whisper
        of Your presence.

Sunlight peeks
  through blushing spring's trees,
    bidding them to awaken
      from a long winter's nap.
        Flowering begins.

Something stirs in me also,
  awakening
    to Your heavenly scent,
while my soul
  nestles into
    the curve
      of Your embrace.
        Flowering begins.

Cate

You were one of the first clear memories
   Of my early childhood.

Your birth and homecoming rode in
   On a celebratory current
     Of newness.
Anticipatory joy
   Framed my little girl existence
As the door opened,
   And you entered.

Ever since, my life has been adorned,
   Marked by your sistering,
    Gifted with your friendship.

My sister . . . one who knows
   And values me so well.

You were one of the first, clear, precious
   Memories of my early childhood.

Little Bird

Little bird up in the sky
I wonder at you, winging high.
Little bird atop the tree,
Do you wonder down at me?

May

May's myriad procession arrives
   regal, on the warm breezes
      of perfumed blossoms.

In her train, petunias and pansies;
   her head crowned with apple blossoms;
      in her hands, a lilac bouquet.

She lingers for a time
   but then must bid adieu
      for other places and springtimes
         that await her presence.

May's royal, myriad procession arrives,
   and awaiting creation curtsies
      to welcome her.

Every May I Remember

Every May I remember the fragrant season of promise
When first I walked in a blossoming time
Carrying a ripened load of life, amidst spring's bright horoscope.

I wondered how my future, our future, would morph and change
Even as my body cradled the life within
That quickened and leapt with such infinite possibilities.

The young woman in me embraced the new
Even as all of nature seemed to anticipate and reflect
The imminent emergence, never before seen.

Oh firstborn of my youth, my heart reflects and muses on it still . . .
For when I birthed you, I too was birthed once again.
Every May I remember.

Flutter-Buzzing

Flutter-buzzing in my ear;
I turned to look, what had I heard?
In splendid beauty, very near
A tiny, regal hummingbird!

Now to the tree he swiftly flew;
I called to him, "Don't go away,
Please do come back!" as if I knew
Some news he held for me, today.

And in response he did return
Flutter-buzzing in midair.
A dear presence from whom I'd learn
To live the day without a care.

Flutter-buzzing in my ear,
My heart now hearing every word.
His presence had to me come near,
A tiny, regal hummingbird.

A Season in My Care

for Stephen

Little boy blond,
asleep in your dreams,
is your sweet life
endless as it seems?

The curve of your cheek,
sweet smell of your hair;
in your tender expression
rests a wee face so fair.

I pause for a moment,
watch your face for a while,
tucking in a round leg;
in your sleep comes a smile.

My heart stares and studies;
I memorize in time
a boy and a baby
for a season in care, mine.

Sleep on, little blond boy,
while night's lit by His star,
for your life and planned destiny
in Love's Hope will live far.

Irene Tree

*Honoring my mother Irene on the anniversary
of her passing before Mother's Day*

Oh, Irene tree,
Lovely and fair,
You wear pink flowers
In your hair.

At every year
About this time
Displaying finery
Sublime,

To honor her
Who gave me birth
You don a veil
Bestowed by earth.

In a few days
Will blow away
Your lovely crown
Arrayed today.

You'll shed your glory
All around;

Petals will fall
Upon the ground.

Still, thank you, tree,
Bequeathing me
The fragrance of
Her legacy.

Thank you, dear one,
Faithful friend
Bloomed every May
Love without end.

I Am Privileged to Live in the Midst of a Bird Aviary

I am privileged to live
   in the midst
     of a bird aviary.

They were here
   before me.

But now
   I am honored
     to dwell in my days
       and evenings
         beneath a canopy
          of sound.

Flying in a time signature
   of grace,
     each has their entry
       into this elaborate chorale
       in layer upon layer
         of colored timbre.

Springtimes

What unseen baton cues them?

An invitation comes to me.

All the clocks
    in the world
        stop . . .
and I am lost
    in the Eden
        of sound.

Spring Cottage

My heart is the place
Where my Jesus will dwell,
A spring cottage in which
His dear secrets He'll tell.

So I'll keep it cleaned up,
Swept out, nothing hide
And there with my best friend
I'll simply . . . abide.

> "The secret [of the wise counsel]
> of the Lord is for those who fear Him,
> And He will let them know His covenant
> and reveal to them [through His word] its
> [deep, inner] meaning.
>
> —Psalm 25:14, AMP

Evening Gratitude

Dusk's spring nocturne draws me
to walk amidst the secrets of evening.
They peek out at me
from adorning shadows.

Her approaching fog mists lightly,
resting upon the subjects
of twilight's benevolent kingdom
gently surrounding me,

and I am grateful.

II. Summering Seasons

Good Night

'Neath twinkling stars
I lay my head
Drifting to sleep
On summer's bed.

June moon above
Fireflies below
Night's lullaby
My heart to know.

Sweet dreams shall come
Turn off the light
Love covers me
And now . . . good night.

Hello Dear Summer

Hello dear summer, welcome here.
My lovely friend, you have come near.
I feel your touch upon my face,
Your friendly breeze, a warm embrace.
I've waited for you all year long.
At last your birds herald your song.
Thank you, my summer, come to me.
Restore my soul and humbly be
My seasoned friend and so revive
My aged youth, ever alive.

And Summer

And summer makes her entrance
upon the gentle breeze
while fireflies bow down to her
and flit around her knees.

Summer Moment

I breathe you in,
Oh summer air.
Upon the porch
Without a care,
I sit, take in
The heart of you . . .
My soul lingers,
Refreshed anew.

Entry Point

My blue kayak is my entry point,
My path into the world of
The Adirondack waterway.
She knows well the way
Far beyond the realm of human rule
Where dragonflies greet and guide
To a place beyond the veil of the wondrous.
As we move across the surface
Of a tannic acid underwater kingdom,
I trust that we will reach our destination
In the land of loons, herons, fish, ducks,
And creatures I've yet to meet.
Time is measured by paddling and discovery
And moments of still magnificence
That etch on the camera
Inside my memory's imagination.
My blue kayak is my entry point,
My path into the world
Of the Adirondack waterway.
She knows well the way.

Adirondack Woods

Speak to me, woods!
Of long summer nights
Beneath your boughs,
While I lie back
Gazing up at your star-bedecked sky,
Breathing in balsam dreams
As nocturnal loons call to me
Across the dark waters.

Sing to me, woods!
As your creatures
Nest in your hair
And coo to my soul.

Cover me, woods!
While I rest in your breezes,
Surrounded by your guarding sentinels,
Soothed by your scents,
Whispered to by your nuances,
While I try to capture these moments
With my feeble words.

But, oh, speak to me, dear woods . . .
Ever so wondrously,
My gentle earth friend . . .
And I will listen.

My Firefly Friend

My firefly friend
    is such a dear sight.
He comes by to visit
    in the summer night.

Carries his lantern
    on his handsome tail
to attract the fancy
    of flying females.

Winging high upward
    on breezes afar,
he shimmers in wonder,
    becoming a star.

My firefly friend
    is enchanting delight.
He comes near to visit
    in the summer night.

Encounter at Montario Point

I happened on him, wondrously;
Great blue heron, in front of me.
At water's edge, 'midst green retreat,
He paused for me, our eyes to meet.

And then in rich, regal display
Spread his great wings
And flew away.

Loons

Loons are calling in the night.
I hear them but they're out of sight,
beneath the gray and purple sky,
my soul connecting with their cry.

Loons' echoes piercing from afar
across the water, 'neath the stars.
They call to me beyond the deep,
speak to my heart in peaceful sleep.

For Danny, Summer 1978

Little boy,
whose short legs love to run
in backyard's grass,

I watch you,
in diligent observation
of the older children,

and realize
the days of your reliance on me
are numbered.

For soon
other lessons and other times
shall mold you
and teach you,
as now only I do . . .

Oh, my wee wise one,
how can one so little possess so much?

Let me cling to this moment
and hold you now
for all of those
in which I won't be able to . . .
tomorrow.

July Musings

Sometimes on a July afternoon,
I enter the women's bathhouse
   On a timeless beach
      And forget what year it is.
Am I nine or seventeen or thirty-three or sixty-five?

What does it matter?
The look, the smell, the familiar memory,
The delicious feeling of the air
   On my drying skin
      After swimming . . .
It is really just all one endless summer of my life.

Sometimes on a July afternoon
When I enter a women's bathhouse,
I forget what year it is.

Eyes of Earth

Evening mist
  rises from the water's surface
    as sunshine's warmth
      focuses on the cooling,
        glistening lake.

I imagine this is
  how it looked in the beginning
    when Your loving breath
      kissed the earth's surface,
        causing the morning mist
          to arise from her dear
            upturned face.

Her eyes met Your gaze
  and earth adored You.

Tonight, the mountain lake's mist
  dances upward
    and worships You
      once more.

I, too, cannot resist, as
  my eyes are drawn higher
    and meet
      You.

Lake Storm

Across the lake she comes
riding upon the abrupt silver winds,
pushing the racing whitecaps
atop the crest of the swirling deep
while the shore's wild upturned leaves
give warning.

The thick haze of mountain rain
is her regal train
and climaxes in an instant,
like a summer curtain
slamming closed the sunbeam window
so earth may be intentionally cleansed.

. . . and the high peaks watch.

Myriads of Meteorites

The backbone
   of the night sky
      is Your footstool.

Myriads of meteorites
   bow down,
      shedding their splendor,

and in their wake
   illuminate the trail
      of Your train

while the morning stars
   sing to You,
      oh, voice of the nova.

Grass Point Portrait

by the St. Lawrence

Plump and robust,
   August croons
      her ripened song

'neath quarter-moon
   hanging
      as a Chinese lantern
         in the sky

while crickets' melody swells
   in harmonic convergence,
      their hearty composition
         an ode to sunset,

and daylight sips her final moments
   like a fine wine,
      sweet and lush
         beneath the
            rising stars.

Firefly Sanctuary

Wanderlust calls
and my childlike heart
responds instantly to the invitation.

Off into the wonderment I go,
pulled into the magnificent realm
of the fireflies.

They escort me into their dimension,
bobbing, weaving, darting in unison
through the refuge of the woodlands
bordering my backyard in enchantment.

Wanderlust calls.
Off into the wonderment I go,
savoring summer's perfume
and taking in this moment of
supernatural light display
I never want to forget . . .
in a firefly sanctuary.

Front Porch at Half-Moon

Portrait of Katie

Little one,
   with eyes so big
      they can hold all the world
         within them,

you try, with utmost intensity,
   to take it all in,
      watching lights and cars
         and life go by.

My longed-for wee girl
   upon my lap,
      you pay attention
         to this summer day,

studying how very much
   can be held
      in simple moments.

And in the midst of such
   supreme effort
      you remain outwardly expressionless
         as to what wise determination
            you have made
               of your observations.

The Beckoning

Eleven PM,
and I follow the beckoning to the nocturnal world
of the shadowed yard that waits for me
when the sun has closed its eyes.

An escort of lightning bugs welcomes me,
as I am flanked by their visual symphony.

Silver moonlight through the woods
sparkles on pool water,
displaying an illuminated bottom
of a silent, mystical world
gleaming, 'neath the translucent surface of this
enchanted moment.

Moon shadow splashes on earth behind me,
as above and around me,
the night adores He
who rides on its breezes
in this summertime, supernatural encounter.

August

August
Sultry, humid
Coming, going, gone
Like a ripened fruit
Deep summer

Full-Term

Last day of summer and
    I muse on the breezes . . .
like the Spirit who blows
    wherever He pleases.
A new sadness abides
    as her exit draws near.
Summer's ripened presence
    has now been fulfilled here.
And I sense her travail
    to bring about new birth
as faint signs of autumn
    appear now on the earth.
We embrace this last day,
    she bears down with her all,
and in just a few hours
    she will birth newborn fall.

III. Times of Autumn

September Woods

I step into the woods,
wandering away
from the harsh glare
and ceaseless noise
of the nine-to-five world.

Each swish, swish, swish
through September's leaves
transports me through
a portal of colorful wonder,

where I sense the kind welcome
of the trees, drawing me near.
They seem to be glad
for me to be there with them.

Now, time is somewhere far away.
I stop,
breathe in the aroma of earthy life,
and wait . . .

Ever so slowly
becoming aware
something is uncurling
on the inside of me.

Could it be my soul
stretching out
like a shy child,
waking up?

Times of Autumn

I linger . . . in luxurious silence
paying attention
for a sign
in this moment where
all things are made new.

The forest floor
seems to take on
a life
all its own,
in a community
of gentle activity.

I marvel. My heart is smiling.

My senses full,
a swish, swish, swishing
carries me back
to the woodland's edge.
My eyes close.
I breathe in
to savor and remember.

I thought surely
I would hear the trees
speaking to me.

Perhaps I just did not stay
long enough.

Raining Leaves

Raining leaves, winding leaves,
   Swirling,
     Twirling down.
Flying leaves dance with ease,
   Gold
     Playing
       All around.
Autumn moving leaves in air,
   Touching down without a care,
Sowing into waiting earth
   Their silent song
     With rustic mirth.
'Tis not their end, this majesty;
   Come spring again, new green will see
     The birthing of their prodigy
       And worth.

October Night Song

Woodland maestro dons baton,
raises it up . . . the music's on.

Evening symphony's delight
in yonder forest 'neath moon's light.

The rising swell of crickets' sound
crescendoing with the trees around,

and now it echoes on the breeze
where fawns recline 'midst colored leaves.

October night song takes a bow;
I raise my glass to toast her now,

so honored just to lend an ear
to wondrous music happening here.

For soon the sounds will cease to be;
they will no longer sing for me.

But still for now I'll linger here,
diminuendo nowhere near.

Now woodland maestro dons baton,
raises it up . . . the music's on.

Somehow, I Have Always Known You

for Dick

Romance of my childhood,
   Somehow, I have always known you.

Love of my youth,
   Somehow, I have always known you.

Faithful companion of my growing-up years,
   Somehow, I have always known

The curve of your face,
The taste of your lips,
The affection of your gaze,
The fire of your desire.

Oh soulmate of my life,
   Somehow I have always known
      The passion of your spirit

In this time . . . and in the next,
   Wedded to mine.

Oh husband of my days,
   Promised one of my heart,
      Somehow, I have always known . . .

You.

Times of Autumn

His Face

I stroke
   the curve of his face,

a sensitive sculpture
   for me to touch
      in tenderness.

Autumnal Procession

Autumn, her subtle arrival unannounced,
is passing through.
With copper golden radiance adorning her face,
crowned and fully seasoned,
she approaches midlife.

A sentinel V of wild geese is moving, skyward, in their ranks.
Something told them it is time to go
as currents of mounting leaves
in a flourish of swirling winds
bid them farewell.

Ageless,
the gracious bounty of ripened blessing
tumbles from autumn's swollen apron,
Thanksgiving trailing in her glory,

while the Ancient of Days presides
over the procession,
witness of such equinox splendor,
and smiling in face-creased approval.

Little Patrick

The smile in my heart,
the poetry of my life
are residing in you.

My autumn days are pavilioned
by your laughing eyes,
encircled by your reaching
little arms,
my soul made light
looking upon your dimpled cheeks.

I see you
and all the sweetness of life
becomes real.
I hold you and I feel rich with meaning.
You look at me
and all the hope of life tells me
it is still mine.

Oh, little Patrick,
when God gave birth to you, out of me,
He birthed me too,
once again.

Wonder

Under the full moon of the midnight hour,
   I wander into the backyard night
      and halt . . .

hearing the sound of leaves tipping, tapping,
   touching onto the October earth's floor,
      splashed in silver.

The moment takes my breath away.
   I have never before heard this ceremony.
      The shadows genuflect, in rapt attention.

I sense the presence of awed night creatures
   in the nearby woods.
      Are they perchance stopping
         to hear the leaves falling, too?

I wonder.

Times of Autumn

Alex, Come and Rest a While

for Cate and Alex the Dog

Alex, come and rest a while;
Wag your tail and make me smile.
Do that thing you always do
That made me give my heart to you.

Snuggle close, forever friend,
Forehead to forehead, never end . . .
So someday in the depths of fall,
I'll feel you never left . . . at all.

Alex, come and rest a while;
Wag your tail and make me smile.

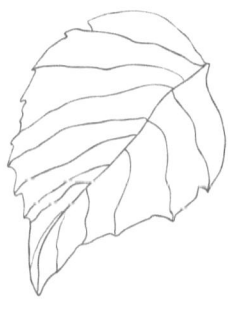

Solitary Star

Solitary star
   rises up
      in the heavens,
a stellar brooch
   to pin
      the cascading mantle
         of eventide.

And I marvel.

He Rides on the Night

He rides on the night,
winds beneath His feet . . .
stars adoring the one
who breathed them into being
with a word.

Water laps upon the shore
  in praise
    in praise
      in praise
knowingly obeying.

Balsam scent wafts upward,
attracted to His presence.
My heart, too, is drawn in
and lifts a song to the sky,

in adoration of He
who rides on the night.

Majesty

A land of distant majesty
on the horizon speaks to me
'neath golden sky beyond the light
with clouds up high beyond my sight.
On river's bank the green spires stand
and guard the way across the land.
And I am welcomed to this scene
where my true heart's been found, serene.

Times of Autumn

For Kevin

Under my roof for one last time,
my youngest son, once baby mine,
who soon will be a bridegroom true,
where one will be what once was two.

Sleep well my son, a man you are.
My heart goes with you, traveling far.
I loved you, reared you for this time,
and you no longer now are mine.

But really, truly never were . . .
You came through me to go to her.

And so, I bless you as you go
unto your bride to live and grow.
Go forth in love and with her be
fulfilled in your bright destiny.

The Piano

My son helped me push the piano to the curb tonight. The disposal service said they will send a special truck for it tomorrow.

It has stayed in our garage for two months while I hoped other arrangements would emerge to adopt it, repair its injuries, and enjoy it as we did for twenty-seven years. That did not happen.

And so, I feel like I am burying an old friend. I laid my hands on it at the curbside and thanked it for the years of little fingers banging on it, growing fingers practicing on it, my fingers rolling over its voice blending with my own, in praise or despair or thanksgiving.

Memories were made possible by it with nights of my husband's Beatles' songs or of Grandpa masterfully weaving his magical audible monuments on it, the final time he came to visit.

I called my daughter tonight. I told her, "We're sending the piano away tomorrow." It was the piano I prayed for, hoped for when I could not afford to buy one. So, I babysat this one. The short-term arrangement became a long-term one, with the family instrument finally bequeathed to us.

I played one last, quiet tribute on it at the curb, tonight. My husband joined in with a celebratory rendition of a Beatles' song offering. Then came a loud, awkward, honoring silence.

Finally, the broken words rose in my throat and fumbled out of me . . . "Thank you, God, for the years with this noble friend that brought so much life to our homes. We now return it to You."

Then I heard myself adding, "Maybe the disposal man will know someone who needs an old friend with a few broken keys."

Into Their Times

Tearfully grateful
   to have known
      the privilege

of a full and bustling household
   that seemed like
      it would never end,

I draw on rich memories now,
   in a season
      replete with imagery
         ever living on

of the bustling household
   of yesteryear,

and the lives
   that went forth
      into their times.

IV. Winterings

Christmas Lights

Old-fashioned
   Glow of lights
      In obscure places

Announces Christmas's approach
   When illumination heightens
      The everyday ordinary
         Into the glorious.

Even in a darkened hallway
   With one Noel candle present,
      Heaven and nature sing.

Tale of Timothy

Child of mine,
   you are moving
      so actively
         inside of me.
I wonder
   what are you thinking,
      dreaming of
as you turn and roll,
   leap and frolic?

From one side to the other
   in the vast universe
   of the height, breadth, and depth
   of my womb,
      you stretch, live,
      and have your being.

My little one,
   my third,
   but always the first
to live this secret
   wonder-filled time with me,

My heart embraces, connects with you,
oh, dear December child of mine.

Adirondacks in Winter

I never knew that I would fall in love
with the Adirondacks in winter,
always having been impassioned by them
in the fully ripened summer.

But today I encounter their wild spirit
to be personally comforting
yet primally challenging.

Brisk air on my face
refreshing my lungs, resuscitating me
while I forest bathe in solitude
is such a good soul tonic.

The mountains put back into me
the wonder of life.
Their people inspire me
with fellowship along life's way,
as I make my discoveries here
with words, with my mind's photographs
... with deep gratitude
for the Adirondacks in winter.

Without a Sound

Tender dancers
twirl in air,
falling snowflakes
everywhere.

Decorating
in the night,
gentle angels
taking flight . . .

Delicate, they
tumble down
and touch my soul
without a sound.

Jack the Cat

My forehead to your forehead,
Pressed together,
In a present momentary knowing of each other;
Your warm head upon my chest,
Purring ... with the rhythm of my breathing ...
Companion.
My finger upon your silky paw,
Your aging face focused, looking into mine,
And I sense
Your faithful, simple kitty-cat soul,
Dear Jack.

Into the Winter Woods

'Midst the loudness of silence
they come.
Poetry in slow motion,
they halt in attention,
at the twenty-first hour
under night's cover.

And everything in me stops,
breathless at the wonder
I witness before me.

I reach behind me
to pull the dark around my shoulders
so deer eyes won't see me
and I can just be with them
in this timeless moment.

Instead, they find me. They study me.
They look into me. They look through me . . .
then satisfied, move gracefully,
magnificently, in slow-motion poetry,
under night's cover, back into the winter woods.

Hope Lay Just Below

January day. And the newly reveling snowflakes meet with the crunchy coldness below.

The oracle within my heart remembers a thousand other Januaries of childhood, when hope lay just below the crusty snowbanks, waiting for a spring thaw to release her from hibernation.

And my memories remind me that the days and nights will melt and flow unabashedly into the light of living.

Even on this January day.

Winter Sketch

Written as a newlywed in early days . . .

January winter evening.

The wind rips through the skies
   as snow swirls
      down
         the
            streetway.

Inside I sit,
   couch and blankets
      curling around me,
paper and pen
   snuggled on my lap,

Invisible radio chattering
   and the oil lamp
      illuminates the corner,

Waiting for my love
   to come home.

Beneath January's Moon

One AM tiptoes in elegant silence
   along the snow's wintry foundation.

So do the deer, gently stepping
   amidst nocturnal pilgrimage.

And the green-boughed bushes
   surrender themselves freely
      to the frigid appetites
         of the nibbling herd of seven.

All is quietly well
   beneath January's moon.

Grandchildren Haiku

Dear grandchildren birthed
to my heart bequeathed anew
life's inheritance.

Musings at Midnight

So, "aging is inevitable but growing old is not" has become one of the new themes of my life as of late.

In the final quarter of living in this body, I am being brought to new reckonings of what that life entails. Some of these revelations are gradual and gentle in approach. Others are more abrupt in announcing themselves.

Looking out through these eyes still brings richness and gratitude for so much beauty. Music, poetry, reading, and learning still pass through and exude a voice, a song from this soul.

This heart still gives and receives living, healing embraces that guide and empower life journeys.

I feel like the little girl I have forever been on the inside. She hears, tastes, smells, touches, feels, laughs, and sorrows with life the way she always has.

Yet late at night as this body rests, I stop to study a hand that looks like one of a woman much richer in years than I.

I find myself gazing at a seasoned vein that has meandered in a far-reaching arm to tell an inevitable, ever-developing story. I watch, mesmerized by the faithful pulse, pulse, pulse in it that has always been my time signature.

A warm gratitude slowly spreads out over me like a blanket. The musings of these moments converge inside to bring a singular, uncommon query to consider.

And I wonder . . . have I really been here for that long a time?

"I can do all seasons of life through Christ who strengthens me."

—Inspired by Philippians 4:13 ESV

About the Author

Poet and author Christine O'Riley was born and grew up in Watertown, NY. She has been writing creatively since age eight. She holds a BA in English, cum laude, from SUNY at Brockport.

In 2017, she founded Pencraft, a local creative writers group in the Rochester, NY area.

Christine finds writing inspiration from nature and in the spiritual realm. She also writes about relationships and the changing seasons of life.

In 2021, she was honored with the Purple Dragonfly New Author Award for Excellence in Children's Literature for her first published work, *The Wondrous Story of the Little Shoe*.

Christine is a semiretired RN by profession and a homemaker, mother, and grandmother by choice. She and her summer romance lifeguard sweetheart, Dick, recently celebrated forty-nine years of marriage. They have six adult children, nine grandchildren, soon to be eleven, and are expecting their first great-grandchild.

They live in Gates, New York, with their feline companion, Jack.

Acknowledgments

A sincere thank-you to my family and friends who have encouraged me in the birthing of this book.

To Katie Helfer, my dear daughter, thank you for activating the manuscript to my publishing coach. Your computer expertise is amazing to me.

To Chris McMullen, artist and friend, thank you for dreaming with me and entering the wonder of this book cover.

To Winnie Lyons, thank you for seeing the poet in me.

To Pencraft sister writers, thank you for your glorious feedback and support.

To Heidi Hakes and the book launch team, thank you for believing in this book.

To my husband, Dick, thank you for reminding me that my poetry is meant to be published.

To Inksnatcher, my publishing coach and editor, thank you for everything. It is an honor to work with you.